The Melody Lies In Between

By Meee

The Adventure of Writing Publisher

Publisher

@poetry.by.meee

I found this dusty worn book
Already judged it by its cover
But the story is amazing
    – By Meee

You know what
I would have sorted it all
Into the right category
But sometimes
Life feels just so messed up
Even how we try to categorize it
No one knows what
Would be the next or
What the day would bring
So why not mix it all up
The themes, styles, and types
How would it go
Or where would it go
Is the question
But only at the end
Will It all make sense

Reach

I have been trying to reach for the stars
But the gravity holds me down
I looked through a telescope for the stars
But a photo can't be written down
I closed my eyes to imagine my own stars
But it isn't the same as in the book I had down
So, I searched for the edges of the horizon
But couldn't find where the rainbow starts
I tried to draw the reflection of the horizon
But each line ends up with another start.
I waited till the stars was behind the horizon
But how can I reach the end if don't have a start

Rise

Words have been a chain on me for years
Held me tied up to the wall
The more I tried to break free, the more I disappear
There is light, so far, so cold, is it from the great hall

If I just could stand up, hiding the chains
No one would notice the wall behind me
Papercut dripping words like rain
Maybe it's better to stay where I can't be seen

Don't listen to words I was told
So I didn't but still it cut deeper then a knife
Would you listen if it was the other way around unfold
Let me out, let me free, let me rise

Yesterday I was at the other side of that door
But now back again chained to the wall
1 word 2 words started out like a small bad seed stored

Once again down the stairs I have fallen

Rise

This isn't me, this isn't where I'm supposed to be
Let me out, let me free, oh, no, don't, wait
I won't leave just take this chain off me
Cause for years this is where I used to stay

The words have become the black wall
The chains for the backpack that I'm carrying every day
Does this room have an edge, where I can fall
Disappearing into anxiety, the other line still stay

Rise

The definition of beauty
Is the angle of the view
– By Meee

Love

Love is more than words
– But it can also be a curse
Love is more than an act
– But it has not a manuscript
Love is more than a feeling
– And yet it's the only left
Love is more than a story
– But it has a whole bookshelf

Served Words

You have words
I have words
But the language
Isn't the same
I can sing for you
Or you for me
But it's still not the same
A melody rising
No words
Words are almost like food
We All can say words

But sometimes it's how it's fused
The way it's being served
Like how we spice the senses
Even over prepared with no taste
And yet it was meant to be simple
sometimes too much is going to waste
The tastier it is
the more delicious it sounds
But just don't burn it before it's served
Who likes fried words in a sauce of clouds

Served Words

The Wrong Mirror

Your words are pushing me to the edge
You might not know this little secret from a small bird
But I already got one foot 2 inches over the edge on one
leg
It might be true since it's not only you saying those
words

Waking up this morning, waiting for the ending
What if I just close my eyes one last night/
You're whispering words into the circle around listening
I'm right, you're wrong, or you´re right, they believe
you're right

From top of the bottoms of the bottle to the edge of the
blade
It's just for creating attention is what you said
But how can you see underneath my hood, behind my
display
Am I a reflection of yourself, but doing what you desire
instead

One or two decades of scares later, I'm still hiding be-
hind that cloud
I tried a couple of times to fly to the other side
But your words are still circling around in the cloudy
crowd
Have you found me inside the shadow of that riverside

  The Wrong Mirror

Am I your Cinderella story without your glory
You kept telling that I didn't have your look, your moves
That I didn't belong in your crowd, your cloud, your
story
But you know what, I´m thankful for not ending up in
your shoes

I'm a writer, not a fighter but every day is a battlefield
But where is my gun, I'm so tired of all those words in
the field
Can I step back, get some space but you removed my
shield
I tried to reach out but I stopped, what if what if it's
the truth unsealed

          The Wrong Mirror

I haven't looked in the mirror for years to avoid the
spike
Cause why should I, It's not me that I see in the mirror
I could try to lose some weight, photoshop my skin, my
height
Just to fit in your ideal of what beauty is considered

It's just in your mind, it's not real, it's just imagination
But my feelings do feel real, the scares, the paper cut,
almost had enough
And yet you said that I need a shrink but hey it's your
mind that has a twisted navigation
My cover might look like a children's book but the pages
can be horrorful crushed

          The Wrong Mirror

A new day is like a gift
Wrapped nicely in an empty gift box
But its up to you
How you would fill it
  - By Meee

Bump

For you it might be
A small bump
But for me it's so much
More like a collision

With my hands free
I'm tied to the chair
Screaming speechless
But who hears me

So then I'm smiling
The chains tight around me
Trying reach out for a call
Shot down by fear

Just turn down the volume
If you're listening to me
Maybe we should take a walk
But first you need to find the key

I can't reach the top of the bump
So raising my glass wall
Behind my mirror in a mirror
Of a reflection of a masquerade

Can you find the exit to this maze
For you it might be over in two turn
But for me it's easier if I just roll my dice
And smile when I overcome the bump

Bump

Road Trip

I remember those late days
When days became nights after sunrise
And our road trips from east to west in the moonlight
With the radio playing singing along battle fight

I remember our late conversations
Where we talked about everything and nothing
And our plans basesed on rolling dice
Of where else to go for a ride

I remember the future talk
Without knowing what we have caught
And by time we became more than ourselves
So those nights are pictures on the shelves

I remember the feelings when time changed
While a new picture found its place
And the best road trip is just about to being
But I still don't know where it might be going

Road Trip

Beautiful Horizon

Once upon a time
A little ships was daydreaming
About sailing the big blue sea
Beyond the horizon
To places it never had seen

"I have heard so many stories
Of places and nature, I only have dreamt of"

It said to it self

"One day I will go
One day I will be there
I can't just sit here
I want to explore the horizon
It's so much more than gray and blue"

     Beautiful Horizon

The other ships were laughing at the little ship
and they said

"you can't set sail,
you will drown
The ocean is too deep
And the waves are too high"

"I just want to write at the edge of the horizon
Laying down the words of what I would see,
Who I could meet, the beauty of things and places"

The little ship replied

One day, one of the older ships came up
And listened to their conversation
And it interrupted

          Beautiful Horizon

"You can't see beyond the horizon with broken lenses,
Here take mine, see the horizon through those,
you might be surprised
If you all just could see through mine
You won't be saying that it's just gray and blue
A beautiful opportunity is ahead
And wonderful chances
Just there to be grabbed, like a buffet
So now go and make your own map"

The other ships didn't say anything
They just looked away
And went back to their own docks

 Beautiful Horizon

"But I haven't never really read a map
And now you want me to make my own"

The little ship asked

The old ship quoted

"Never tried
Never failed
If never failed
How will we then learn
If never learned
How would we than know
If we don't know
How can we than evolve"
-By Meee

                    Beautiful Horizon

The little ship was quiet for a bit
Then it looked at the others with a smile
As it began moving away from the dock

"It's a beautiful day today"

It said with a wave
And set sail out of the harbor

Beautiful Horizon

Have you ever
Tried looking
For something
You didn`t know
But figured out
That it was right
In front of you
       - By Meee

Wish For A Wish

Have you
Ever wished
That you could
Wish for a wish
Like wishing
In a wishing well
But the wish
You wish for
Is more than
A wish

It's the wish
That makes
Dreams a reality
And reality dreams
Cause without
That wish
There aren't no
Other wishes
To wish for
But wishes
Don't always come
In the ways that
We wished

          Wish For a Wish

Dear Dairy

How can it be if I break my leg or hurt my arms
It's okay to feel the pain
But when I wish I never had been born
I have to stand up and smile

How can it be that when I had a surgery?
You're asking how am I doing
But if I ask for help for my mentality
It's taboo that you won't be introducing

How can it be I that have to dance at the edge
Before you realize it's more then hide and seek
And yet I had to write in red on the white page
Maybe you should borrow my shoes for a sneak peek

How can it be if a shrink gives a disorder
You take a step back to the sideline
But what if you are next in order
Should I hand you a firearm and say welcome to my life

Dear Dairy

Note

Sometimes it can feel easier to die then to live
But what is life if I'm already dead
What if I could watch myself from heaven
Would I go back to pull the trigger to my head

Bury my scrapbook in the back yard
Right underneath my suicide note
To erase every step from existing
For just to take one more round

Is it possible to borrow the gun another day
If this doesn't go as planned
My to do list is longer then my middle finger
Maybe the front yard is better than my back

A robe, a tree maybe one day I could fly
But hey what's the meaning if I end this
Would it be a success or another failure
Is the dream the dream I had dreamt

Can I come to my own funeral
Cause I got some words that I don't want to hear
Hah, and you said I was a good person
But have you seen what's behind the cover

Note

I think it's a ghost wearing my skin
There aren't any reflection in the mirror
Am I locked behind the broken glass
Watching myself but no one hear me screaming

Why would you listen, I wouldn't listen to myself
So why should you when I couldn't
A scare or ten to get my own attention
New red paint dripping but try calling next week

Note

But what if this is the end, the edge
I know I have been dancing on the edge of that blade
But unfortunately, it hasn't got me yet
Maybe one day I will be my own headline

Is dying the meaning of living
Or is it the end for a new beginning
But how do I know that life isn't just an illusion
A dream that has become a nightmare

Note

If monsters were more than a fairy tale
How would they then appear
- By Meee

Outside Smiling

So how are you doing
Is a question with the expectation of already knowing

I'm good
I'm great
It couldn't going better
What a beautiful day

But what would you say if I dropped my outside smile
And told you what I have been holding on for a while

I wanna crawl back into bed, to my hideout tent
Bring me my hood, my headphones, you will never
notice me again

I can't be in my own skin, I can't wear this, take it all
away
Draw me a picture of where I can be me, where I'm
more than a play

But since you asked, would you then pick up the phone
when I'm dancing in ashes
Or let it slide to the next with a label saying "looking
fine, just few scratches"

Outside Smiling

Ocean

Have I ever told you
Oh, wait, no, I don't think so,
I have been trying to
But you see, I'm your snow globe

A little shake and I'm already snowing
But this tale is for you
Is more then a globe holding
But how to let out, I never knew

Have you ever noticed my snow globe
It's right here underneath my coat
Not to be shook or shown
An iceberg in the ocean like a Poke

Have you heard, oh I had been whispering
Shaking it, you shaking my world to burn
Untold stories, Sssh but you can't be entering
This is the snow globe of my ocean

Ocean

Mirror

If I just could escape through the mirror on the wall
And go to the hollow side of hopeless reflections
Seeing myself inside another perspective of the guildhall
If this was the dimensions of version with possibilities

Am I at the right path or should I pick a string and
make a butterfly?
To recreate my world in the image that I want it to be
Where the reality isn't more than shelves of fantasies
And the fantasy isn't bound to the reality to be invisible

Mirror, mirror is this me or is my shadow a reverse error
Should I go after the reflection of myself that is expected
Or see through the original vision of version mirror
But escaping through the mirror is another puzzle to be solved

Mirror

Who you are today
Is the scrapbook
Of the journey
You have been through
– By Meee

One Word

Just one word starts a call
I didn't know it would bring another round
Or how it went too far at all
But now it's a fireball coming down
Like heavy rain of ink raining inside my hall
Burning down my whole background
If I just knew it could start in so small
Like whispering to the clouds
My hall, I fall, I'm crawling to the wall
This foundation is thinner than paper sides
Small scratches growing in my redecorated hall
Hit rock bottom by this word of yours

Falling off to fly to the other side of the rainfall

Just one word brought back the colours
I didn't know it was possible to fan the flame
Or how it's can be worth more than dollars
But it feels like the butterflies came
To repaint the ink to a colourful sculpture
Recapturing my background with a green frame
If I just knew how simple this could be at all
Like the rings in the water after a stone dropped
My hall, my wall, I'm rising like a fireball
With a foundation I got rock stocked
And new note poster's redecorating my hall
At the end an unspoken word says more than an spoken

I'm holding the one word in a glass ball

                    One Word

I Tried I Tried

I have tried to awaken this feeling deep inside of me
Like a part of me is missing but which I can't feel
Staring at the ceiling counting down for my other life to
fleet
But I can't remember when the last time my dreams
were sweet

Please don't wake me for another nightmare in the
daylight
Rise and shine or fall and cry, spin which is insight
Your smile, it's so bright that I see the end of the maze
So, so, close and yet so far from the edge of this phase

I tried to get out of the bed this morning
But back to bed, my energy is leaking
The sun hasn't even reached the skyline shining
It's not my sun, mine is hiding, cloudy and raining

If I just could be flying above the line than falling
Hiding behind the clouds waiting for the days without
raining
So much light, too loud, duvet makes me fading
Someone wake me from this nightmare I must be
dreaming

I Tried I Tried

I tried I tried to regain the strength to smile honestly
But it seems to be another bad bedtime story
Where did my energy go with my sanity
Am I hollower than a bottle that is empty

My house has open doors, but no one knows the entry
The walls squeezing around me without any empathy
Am I dreaming, am I screaming, why is this feeling gray
Just let me stay in my bed to get past another day

I Tried I Tried

Home

A home is a home
But without bricks and stone
We rather live in a phone
And yet it's still not the right tone
So do we even have a safe zone
Or is it another imaginary throne
Just to fill out our tombstone
And yet is it enough to fill our homes
So where should we place our cornerstone
It seems that bricks and stones
Can't keep holding on to our home
So, we fell in to the phone zone
To not feel left out and alone
But it does seem unfair and unknown
Is this stronger or more fragile than stone
Who knows where to recharge our home?

The pursuit of the dream
Isn´t always the biggest dream
But the dream for today
– By Meee

Just Words

Can we have conversation in the style of poetry
Without writing down words but rather speak
out what we feel

Having our feelings spoken, seems to be spoken words
supposedly
Just keep the white paper black ink free not to appeal

Could we, should we have an honest conversation
without a gum bubble
How are you, me? I'm fine thanks for the auto reply

Maybe we could turn off the auto correct, auto tune, to
see through the bottle
Come to me again when it's your style, your words
spoken out to apply

Plus Minus =

We are drawing to each other
Like hell and heaven on collision
A game with the wrong lover
And yet we are the perfect audition
A puzzle with just two pieces
But too close we got repulsed
Even that we are Mr. and Mrs.
Plus minus equal trouble
But apart we are yin without yang
How can we hold on without a bag
We are wrapped nicely into a paper swan
And yet we are wearing a dog tag
Our path is a fantasy in a history book
Dreams nightmares walking together
Drawing a picture of how, would, should
Plus minus equal pleasure

A Dreamer's Hopes

I tried once if I could hold on to it
But it's even more slippery than the wind
It did open for emotion more than a bottle ever did
Even removes the sanity and the reality print

Lighting up everything around me like art
And yet blackouts everything else
Sometimes it raising the tempo of my heart
But slowing down the surroundings breaths

A Dreamers Hopes

Almost like a poison that is stronger than the blue pills
And yet it's sweeter than honey in a snack box
An addiction of the highest price but with priceless bills
Confused and yet more clear then my inbox

It made me into a speechless speaker
Without words written down in my letters
If I just could hold on to it rather then another swiper
But how do I dare to reach it than being a checker

     A Dreamers Hopes

Sometimes we
Forgot to see
The beauty
In the smallest
Details of the
Bigger picture
-By Meee

Hallo

Hallo
How are you?
I'm fine thanks or am I wrong to your according
But It's you who I have been talking to
Telling me how I am doing feeling thinking
By the way who are you
How can it be that your voice speaks louder then mine?
And yet it's easier to listen your words review
I even don't know how you got comfortable and settled down
Oh well, you can call me your friend from long ago
But I'm going under many names when I appear
All I did was plant a seed for my tree house to grow
And see us now, I have become your happiness and fear

Chasing

Chasing to capture the beauty of the wilderness
So, it can make us wonder how beautiful it is

But what about the backstage of the picture
Chasing the beauty in nature but end up with
stages filters

The real beauty is now the edited version of nature
Like the reality captured in a studio

A wild forest cut to figure into the right texture
And yet we wonder at the beauty through the window

What If

What if the world was flat?
And the moon was glass

What if war and love walked hand in hand
Where would hope than stand

What If there was peace?
Would jealousy appear

With jealousy would there be hate
From hate war might be awake

What if dreams
Came true by believes

What if the reality was the illusion?
And the illusion is the solutation

And what if what we're seeking
Isn't what we are really believing

But the satisfaction we are needing
To keep up the daily smiling

What If

Emotion is like an outfit
There is an outfit for every single occasion
And yet we are wrapped like a gift
To fit the daily expectation
– By Meee

Dear Demon

For so long I want to write you a letter
But now it's maybe a bit too late

I should care but I don't as I used to
Before I was a figure in the shadow of you

But still I'm trying to find myself
Inside the maze that you have trapped me in

Even your friends from underneath my bed are in here
Like I'm a bait hunted through the halls and the walls

You gave me a knife a rope and a tree
Go play with this, you encourage me to

Dear Demon

But if you ever read this, I just want to tell you
That I'm escaped, out of your spiderweb, for you it's too
late

Now I'm my own star not the one that you had hope
for
Even though you tried to consume my soul make, me
hollow

Left me in the dark to the shadows
Let's bring the edge of your timeline closer, was your
words

But now I found the spark and ignited it
So yeah, now it's time for you and I to part

But just one last thing, maybe this wasn't a part of your
plan
But it is mine, your lesson taught me how

Sincerely

Dear Demon

Passing Through

Hey, hello, how are you
I'm just passing through
Have you even noticed my footprint along yours?
I might leave you sticky notes on the floors
But what's written is up to you
It's on your floor so I have placed it in the queue
Did I give or take, A least I got some memories
With a scrapbook of us saved for centuries
But will I ever get a space in your hall of names
Or am I still a traveler no matter the miles, our lines
Oh well I'm just passing through
Been a pleasure to meet you

Story Time

Can I tell you a story about that guy?
With the hood that covered the reflection of the sky

Telling the truth was another lie meeting halfway
But every night he was praying, waiting "come and take me away"

It seems easier to play with a knife then open the door
And yet he wasn't ready but still standing on the trapdoor

Instead, he was drowning in booze to forget his
backpack
Even In the mirror he was invisible to be backtracked

Opening his arms to try to remove the pain underneath
In the end he ends up being his own grand Masterpiece

Have you heard the gossip about that girl?
She's from the suburbs but that seemed burned

                    Story Time

She could have been the model on a cover of a magazine
But ends up in the obituaries on the last scene

The appetite was water and some gum
While she was seeking love to not feel numb

With closed eyes she whispered loud
"Now I'm ready to learn how to fly out"

How could she ever rebuild her image?
Retake the restored memories from the other side of
that bridge

Story Time

If we keep
Writing, talking, reading
The same way
As we always have
How do
We than know
If we had learned
- By Meee

Anxiety

What if I just for once
Could grab the chance
And open the door to the front
For so long I have been hiding behind my rhymes

I have been settled down and became comfortable in
here
Walking out that door and leaving this room, this safety
zone
Maybe the window is the fastest way down, escaping the
fear
Or have I become a memory of a portrait I had known

What would I have missed if I opened the door one day
Walking outside against the inner voices in the clouds
All these eyes staring at me, even though they aren't
looking my way
But still whispering all around me, too many, a crowd,
too loud

They all can hear me whispering out loud, can I crawl
back and hide
Take me back to my hideout, my door, my bathroom
floor
I can breathe now, no one sees me, hears me, let me
stay inside
But is this where I'm supposed to be, inside these walls
of four

                                        Anxiety

Uphill slope

It's might a uphill slope
But I will see sunrise above
Touching the stars at the top
But is it really enough

I won't back down
Maybe I should go higher
Up where I can't drown
Am I my own survivor

Or have I been pushed up
A hand from each I meet
The uphill slope might suck
But who knows what's next

At least I got my own top
Can't be pushed back now
But I will remind my drops
And see, it's not always night

Uphill Slope

Flower

A flower was enjoying the sun
When a bee flew by
And landed on the next flower
A few days passed, the bee kept passing by
But it didn't land on this flower once

"Why won't you visit me"
The flower asked

"You got no sweetness in you
so I have no use for you"
The bee replied

A few weeks went by
While the bee was laughing at the flower
One day the bee landed on the flower

                                    "Why are you still here
                                Your type isn't even near
                             Maybe I should find you a deer
                              Cause all you give me is tears"
                                               The bee said

The flower didn't know what to say
So it closed its leaves
The other flowers turned and asked

                              "Why are you closing your leaves
                               Those words can't be believed"

                                      "But the bee it's right
                                         I'm not like you

It's a lie for me to even have tried
I will always be your emo"
The flower replied

                    Flower

The other flowers continued

"Please open up your leaves
So we can enjoy the view of you
It's the bee who is the thief
Not you, you're a beautiful view

Have you even seen you, you're a rose
We are just a wild mix of flowers
Standing in this field feeling disposed
But you make us forget our desires

Having you here makes our day fulfilled
Without you we would just be yellow and green
So you see, you're a part of this field
Please feel free and be the flower you're meant to be"

                    Flower

Moments are like stones
They come in many shapes and sizes
They are heavy and yet
They can be fragile
- By Meee

Writers Block

I'm just a writer trying to put words down
And thoughts drawn on the paper white
But I don't know how to draw beautiful lines
Can I paint with more than one color and use them all

But I'm even worse to start a conversation with real
words
Trying to speak but can't find the right word to say
So I end up being a bit goofy
With words and sentences that makes no sense

So I'm staring at the emptiness while thoughts are pas-
sing by
If I just could reach out to tie them down
But I can't hold on, they are too slippy, too many
The writers block, stocked as the words ran off

Is it the white line, a lifeline, redline, timeline
Or It's just another empty line that I got to fulfill
Which words should I use or should I just catch them as
they comes
But should I write a poem or a lyric with some rhymes

Writer Block

Where it all ends on the same
Or have a word game
With a prize that we can claim
So we can hang it in a frame

But hey, we will have to wait to see what's it's going to
be
I'm not done yet, I'm just stocked in my boat
With a handful of words that should have been drawn
On to the empty line to rewrite the writers block

Writer Block

Piece

I shouldn't be anyone else but me
But my piece doesn't seem to fit in
Am I in the right place to be
Or are they not ready for what I'm holding in?

Fading

I should held you tight
When I was holding your hands

You melted my heart on the white paper night
What you and I caught was the beginning of the end

All this was for us but I forgot to be there for us
You're my star, I reached out, so close and yet so far,
slipping away

And now I'm left behind your tail of star dust
If I just held you tight more than nights, would you had
stayed

If time were just an illusion
And the end the only option
Is fantasy then the limits
And reality a sentence
– By Meee

I Got Told

Take a pen and write down your past and your feelings
But hey, do you wanna see my scrapbook, am I your
storyteller, it's my fairytale
Where I'm from doesn't matter for where I'm going
I'm might come from the mountains pass but I'm
heading for sea to set sail

Do you also want my burned resume but I can't pick the
ashes
The road behind me might have formed me to the one I
am today but it's not my definition
Sorry I didn't grow up like you so does it mean that I
should write a suicide notes
How can my picture background describe my vision for
the next destination

Chance

Taking the first step
Into the mist
Is a leap of faith
With closed eyes
What happens next
Is experience
But a nightmare
If not the chance has been taken

Between The Lines

You have already been at my line
Dancing all night till breakfast at nine
And yet we ended it all too soon
Didn't got a chance to show that this is more than car-
toon

Maybe you would come again to my paper house
And we could pick a new line to announce
Just don't go into my locked room
It's just like a diary, a little notebook I assume

Okay, okay, come and read my white paper wall
It has been written with eyes closed in the great hall
Let me know if you can read the invisible red ink
I have tried to find it to rewrite it for another drink

But I didn't get any color book, so this is painted in
black and white
Maybe you could bring some more colors next time we
swipe
And than we could play hide and seek in between the
words
The winner can draw our own fireworks afterwards

     Between The Lines

I'm sorry I'm not used to visitors at my paper house
page
It's just easier to close it all in like a book edge
Having you here on my line isn't what I'm familiar with
It's almost like having a private show with you on my
VIP list

The title on this cover should have been night and day
But black and white, you mixed it to be gray
So all I can say is welcome to my mixed up page
Words after words, written wall turned into a new
stage

Between The Lines

Words can be spoken
And yet not be heard
Words can be written
And yet not be seen
Words can be so much more
And yet they are being taken for granted
            - By Meee

Coin of One

All I want was to write you
Lay down a letter with words that may not sound new
But I just try to write above my writer's block
Or am I over thinking the sentence till it's locked

How about we sit down over a home cooked meal
And after a couple bottles of wine, we can tell how we
feel
I wish I knew what I want to say to your face
But telling you my tale could end up being A waste

Cause it seems that I forgot to tell you something lately
You see, I'm grown up now, got my own family
So that means I don't need you like you need me
You hold on to another dream that I ever could see

You were the only voice in my head for way to long
But now we are over and gone
Unfortunately for you I'm not a quitter
I'm still here, still me, still a dreamer

                    Coin of One

Why couldn't you just traveled over seas
Cause this was what we used to but now just memories
Oh well you aren't on my guest list
Maybe on my wish list, hit list, bucket List

And if you would be, you would be marked done
Now you're just a sad story on the shelves dumped
Trying to rewrite the storyline with my pen
But now we aren't the coin of one as we had been

          Coin of One

Drawing

I remember back in school that one day my teacher told
us to

"Draw a picture of yourself
Of how you see yourself
In a 10 years dream of yours
Holding the achievements of yours"

We didn't really know what our teacher meant
So we asked

"How do you want us to make a drawing
Of something that we really only can guessing
It would be like wishing
For something we are dreaming"

"Yes!"

Our teacher responded excited

"That's exactly what you are going to do
No matter what other thinks could be a taboo"

We were a little bit confused, but tried our best to draw
what we were told
But stopped
And asked again

"How, how can we do it right?
How do we know what we are dreaming at night?
What if we want to but fail even before we tried?
Do you think if it's wrong we can overwrite?"

                    Drawing

"Well"

Our teacher took a deep breath and looked at us
And continued

"You see,
Drawing what you dream isn't always just a dream
Sometimes it's become a nightmare
before it can be realized for real
But what I should had said was
Draw a picture of what you like and love cause

Then you would draw a picture of those things
you are doing the most
Maybe it could be a secret you holding close

It could be like
Would it be like

                    Drawing

Dancing like you where on a stage of ballet
or an street performing
Drawing like an artist with the paper and pencil
or is it digital painting

Singing those words and feeling out loud
or moving the universal language speaking
Running faster than lightning
or having the moves while you're jumping

Thinking thoughts in a code no one knows
or speculations about space and time bending
Writing down words to stories to be read
or your fantasy of another reality telling"

Our teacher smiled at us
We didn't say a word
But just listened like it was a storytelling or a movie

                    Drawing

"So therefore for some it might be a little secret to hold
Of who you are and what you like doing
So being creative
Talking with others supportive
Speaking out your heart,
Doing sports in level hard
Or what else could be your deal
There is always a hidden talent underneath
But the specific type doesn't really matter
Because It might change by time after
Just the basic will always remain the same
No matter the ages you hide your game"

I looked down to see my drawing
There was just a couple of smiles and a Meee

Drawing

If

If a myth is a myth, when was the original?
If love can't be felt, why is it that we feel the most?
If dreams are our desire, is it then a nightmare?
If an endless story is endless, when did it start?
If we have someone to listen, why do we speak silence?
If a smile can make the day, what can a hug do?

 Drawing

Publisher: The Advnture of Writing Publisher ApS
www.awpublisher.dk
E-mail: Contact@awpublisher.dk
Auther: By Meee
Formats: Epub and Softcover
ISBN 978-87-974508-0-2

More publication
The Melody of Life, 2022

www.ingramcontent.com/pod-product-compliance
Lightning Source LLC
LaVergne TN
LVHW091511170726
843492LV00001B/438